DISCARD

D1209459

20th Century Inventions
AIRCRAFT

Ole Steen Hansen

RSVP
RAINTREE
STECK-VAUGHN
PUBLISHERS
The Steck-Vaughn Company

Austin, Texas

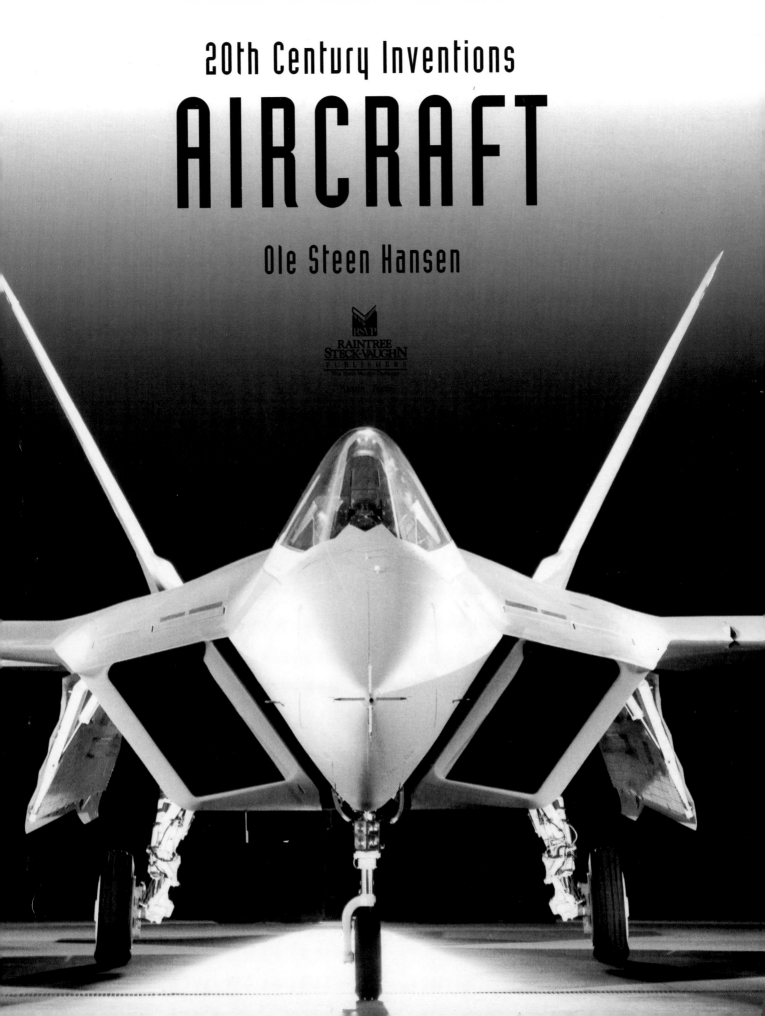

387.73
Han

20th Century Inventions

AIRCRAFT

CARS

COMPUTERS

THE INTERNET

LASERS

MEDICAL ADVANCES

NUCLEAR POWER

ROCKETS AND SPACECRAFT

SATELLITES

TELECOMMUNICATIONS

Front cover and title page: The Lockheed YF-22 Advanced Tactical Fighter

© Copyright 1998, text, Steck-Vaughn Company

All rights reserved. No part of this book may be reproduced or utilized in any form or by any means, electronic or mechanical, including photo-copying, recording, or by any information storage and retrieval system, without per-mission in writing from the Publisher. Inquiries should be addressed to: Copyright Permissions, Steck-Vaughn Company, P.O. Box 26015, Austin, TX 78755.

Published by Raintree Steck-Vaughn Publishers,
an imprint of Steck-Vaughn Company

Library of Congress Cataloging-in-Publication Data
Hansen, Ole Steen.
Aircraft / Ole Steen Hansen.
  p.   cm.—(20th Century Inventions)
Includes bibliographical references and index.
Summary: Presents a basic overview of the history
and development of aircraft, one of the great success
stories of the twentieth century.
ISBN 0-8172-4816-1
1. Airplanes—Juvenile literature.
[1. Airplanes.]
I. Title. II. Series.
TL547.H15   1998
387.7'3—dc21   97-7664

Printed in Italy. Bound in the United States.
1 2 3 4 5 6 7 8 9 0 02 01 00 99 98

Picture acknowledgments
Aviation Picture Library/Austin J. Brown 11 (top), 15 (right), 23 (bottom), 38, 41, 42, 43; Britstock back cover and contents page/Baron Wolman; Bruce Coleman Ltd 23 (top); Deiter Betz 21 (top); John Dale 39; Erik Frikke 17 (top), 35; Ole Steen Hansen 4, 5 (both), 9 (both), 10 (bottom), 12, 13, 15, 16, 17, 18, 21 (bottom), 22, 24 (bottom), 25, 27 (both), 28, 29 (both), 30 (both), 31, 32/British Aerospace Defence, 34, 36, 40 (top)/British Aerospace Defence, 44 (bottom), 45 (both); Rob Hewson front cover and title page, 8, 20, 33, 37, 40 (bottom); Photo Link 6, 7; Plane Picture Company 19. Artwork by Tim Benké, Top Draw (Tableaux). All other pictures Wayland Picture Library.

CONTENTS

9/98 Library Budget 16.98 Follett Library Resources

INTRODUCTION

Aircraft of all shapes and sizes have become part of our daily life. The world's biggest and busiest international airport is London's Heathrow Airport. At the busiest times, an aircraft lands there, takes off, or flies over every 20 seconds. A number of smaller airports are needed to help cope with the huge number of aircraft arriving daily in Great Britain's capital.

A smaller world

The aircraft is one of the truly great inventions of the 20th century. The first flight by a powered aircraft took place in 1903. By 1919 the Atlantic Ocean was crossed, and just 50 years later the world's first supersonic airliner, Concorde, took to the air.

A Continental Airlines DC-10 arrives at London, Gatwick Airport. Hundreds of people have been involved in making sure the passengers had a safe and pleasant flight from Houston, Texas.

Many people make their first flight in a light aircraft. Here a Cessna 150 is being refueled. Like most other aircraft, it has its fuel tanks in the wings.

War in the air

Early aviators realized that their new invention could be used for war. Some imagined that aircraft would make wars so unpleasant that fighting would not take place. Unfortunately, this hopeful view lasted only a short time, because aircraft were used to grim effect during World War I (1914–1918). Since then, nations have used aircraft to wage war, to attack another country without warning, or to secure peace and freedom.

The year 1969 saw another significant event in the history of aircraft with the first flight of the Boeing 747—the jumbo jet. By providing cheap seating for a large number of passengers, the jumbo jet introduced a new age of mass jet transportation. Today, the world's airlines fly more than 2.75 million passengers every day. Traveling over 30,000 ft. (10,000 m) above the ground at 560 mph (900 kph) has become an everyday experience.

Aircraft have made the world appear or feel smaller. A hundred years ago, traveling around the world in 80 days was a major challenge and an experience out of reach of most people. Today, the flight between Los Angeles and Australia takes about 22 hours, and hundreds of thousands of people have flown the route.

The size of Concorde is emphasized by the Mirage 2000 fighters flying next to it. No other airliner crosses the Atlantic Ocean at such a fast speed.

HISTORY

Early aircraft, such as this Avro Triplane, were unreliable, underpowered, and difficult to fly. Aviators learned to fly them largely through trial and error.

In 1903, the American brothers, Orville and Wilbur Wright, designed and flew the first powered aircraft. Wilbur visited France in 1908 and gave a demonstration of flying that helped to speed the development of powered flight in Europe. The following year, an aircraft crossed the English Channel for the first time. However, at that time, the challenge for all aviators remained to stay aloft and, perhaps, to overtake a train if they were flying with a tailwind.

World War I

When World War I broke out in 1914, aircraft still had few practical uses. But that was soon to change. Pilots on both sides flew over battlefields and directed the heavy guns to aim shells at enemy lines. Then some pilots began to drop grenades, steel arrows, and bombs on enemy troops. Others flew with the sole purpose of shooting down enemy aircraft with the rifles and machine guns they carried. By the end of the war, the three basic types of military aircraft—observation aircraft, the bomber, and the fighter—had developed.

The Vickers Vimy was built as a World War I bomber, but its main claim to fame was its record-breaking flights after the war, including the first nonstop transatlantic crossing. This Vimy was built by a joint U.S.–Australian team to reenact and celebrate the first England–Australia flight in 1919. It is shown flying in formation with a Bristol fighter, another famous World War I aircraft.

The pilots escaped the horrific conditions and bloody fighting that were taking place on the ground. Flying in formation with friends in the sunshine above the clouds gave a special feeling that few people had experienced. But there was still a heavy price to pay. Airmen suffered horrendous casualties, and in the darkest days of the war a pilot could only expect to stay alive for three weeks.

The golden years (1919–1939)

Peace was followed by years of adventure and widening horizons. Aircraft had become faster, longer ranging, and much more reliable. Aviators now started to prove that they could fly anywhere. Long-distance pilots became the superstars of the day, and excited crowds would gather to witness another record-breaking aircraft arriving.

If you were well off, you could fly to Australia in a few days— a journey that would take weeks by ship. Compared with modern jets, airliners were slow, noisy, and uncomfortable. But at the time they were the height of modern technology.

Aircraft could carry mail too, and this paved the way for new long-distance postal services. For example, in 1924, the U.S. Post Office began an air mail service between the cities of New York on the east coast and San Francisco on the west coast. The flight was flown in relays and took about 30 hours if the winds were favorable.

WORLD WAR II

The Flying Fortress was the main U.S. bomber over Europe in World War II. Battles involving more than a thousand bombers and fighters frequently took place in the skies over Germany. Never before and never since have aerial battles been on a scale like that.

Aircraft became decisive, war-winning weapons in World War II (1939–1945). During the first two years of the war, bombers and fighters spearheaded the German army's advance across Europe. But by winning the Battle of Britain in 1940, the Spitfires and Hurricanes of the RAF saved England from a German invasion. In 1941, a surprise Japanese air attack on the U.S. Pacific Fleet in Pearl Harbor in Hawaii brought the United States into the war.

By 1943, heavy, four-engined British and U.S. bombers were destroying city after city in Germany. In the last year of the war, fast, low-flying fighter-bombers roamed over the battlefields of Europe, making it almost impossible for the Germans to move tanks and men in daylight.

After a total German defeat, two nuclear bombs ended the war in Asia. A U.S. B-29 bomber dropped the first bomb on the Japanese city of Hiroshima on August 6, 1945. Eighty thousand people were killed instantly. A second bomb over Nagasaki three days later finally forced Japan to surrender.

Hundreds of thousands of aircraft were built during the war. But most of them were out of date as soon as the war ended. The jet engine had been invented, and a new age of flight was about to begin.

Jet-powered airliners

The jet engine heralded a new era in civil aviation. First flown in 1954, the Boeing 707 became the world's first truly inter-continental jet-powered airliner. Jets flew twice as fast as other types of aircraft and gave a much smoother flight because they vibrated less. They flew high above most of the gusty weather and air currents that often made flying uncomfortable. This Boeing 707 is still in service in Spain and is seen here taking off with government officials for a United Nations summit meeting in 1995.

The Cold War

During World War II, the United States and Soviet Union had both fought against the Germans. But when peace returned, the two countries were each afraid that the other might attack, and they became hostile to each other. The world became divided as many countries sided with either the United States or the Soviet Union. This period lasted until 1989 and is known as the Cold War, since there was no large-scale fighting between the two sides.

The Cold War set off an arms race as both sides strove to build the best and most powerful weapons in order to deter the other side from attacking. Jet engines made it possible for aircraft to fly higher than ever before and faster than the speed of sound. Almost all military aircraft in service today were designed as part of the Cold War arms race.

The Canberra jet-bomber first flew in 1949 and served with the RAF during most of the cold war in a great number of roles, including top-secret spy flights over the Soviet Union. This Canberra is being refueled by an RAF ground crew.

WINGS

Gravity is the force that attracts things to the earth and causes them to fall to the ground. Aircraft need wings to overcome gravity and stay up in the air. "Lift" is the term used to describe the upward force that allows an aircraft to fly.

Lift

Lift is created when the wing moves forward through the air. Most lift is created by a low-pressure area forming over the top surface of the wing (see diagram below). The wing is "sucked" rather than "pushed" up into the sky. The larger the wing, the more lift is created. And the faster the air flows over the wing, the more lift there is, too. In fact, the amount of lift is increased four times by doubling the speed of the air flow.

The air passing over the curved upper surface of the wing moves faster than the air passing under the flat lower surface. A low-pressure area is created above the wing and this creates lift.

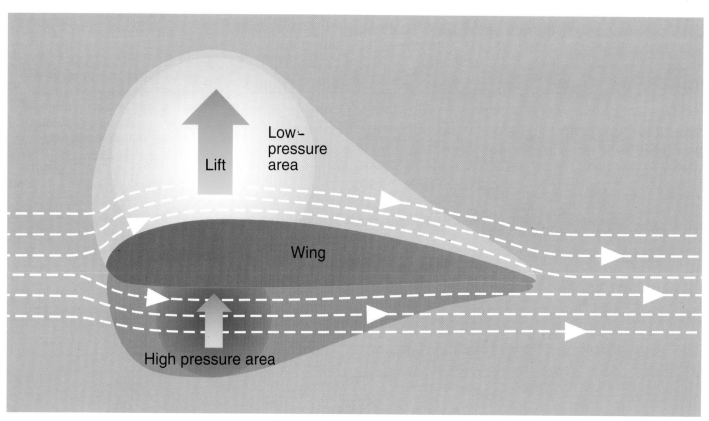

Lift

Low-pressure area

Wing

High pressure area

A U.S. Navy F-14 Tomcat with its flaps extended seconds before touchdown. The arrester hook catches a wire laid across the deck of the aircraft carrier to help the aircraft stop in the small landing space available.

The right wing for every occasion

Some military jets, such as this F-14 Tomcat, have swing wings. When flying fast, little lift is needed, so the wings are backswept and form a delta shape similar to the wings on Concorde. At slower speeds —for takeoff and landing— more lift is needed, and so the wings are used in the forward position. This position is also used in combat when the aircraft is pulled through tight turns.

Early aircraft had weak engines, flew slowly, and needed large wings to create enough lift for them to fly. A modern Boeing 737, despite being ten times as heavy as the Vickers Vimy (see page 7) when loaded with fuel, 150 passengers, cargo, and luggage, has a smaller wing than the Vimy because it is able to cruise at around 560 mph (900 kph).

Flaps

The small wing of a jet airliner was ideal for cruising at speed at high altitude. However, unless the shape of the wing could be altered in some way, the airliner would be difficult to land safely, as the landing speed would need to be very high to create enough lift. Flaps on all modern aircraft solve this problem by making the wing more curved, or cambered, which increases the lift. The flaps also increase drag, which help slow the aircraft. A Boeing 737 usually lands at around 146 mph (235 kph) with its flaps fully extended. Without flaps it would have to land at 208 mph (335 kph).

The passengers' view of the fully extended flaps of a jumbo jet about to land. The flaps enlarge the wing area by 20 percent and create 80 percent more lift.

JET ENGINES

Piston engines, broadly similar to car engines, are used in small aircraft. In airliners and military aircraft, jet engines are used. The development of the modern jet engine made possible the construction of today's big jets. A jumbo jet would have needed eighteen of the largest piston engines ever built to get airborne.

Some aircraft use a type of jet engine in which the power is used to turn a propeller. This is known as a turboprop engine. Turboprops are very cheap to run on smaller airliners. The Jetstream on page 24 is powered by turboprops.

How modern jet engines work

The basic principles of a jet engine are simple. Air is sucked in at the front and squeezed, or compressed, before it enters a chamber called the combustion chamber. There fuel is burned, which causes the air to expand and force its way out through the exhaust at the rear of the jet engine.

Two Boeing 737s. The Air France has the older turbofan engines. The Braathens has the modern high-ratio bypass turbofans, which have a much larger air intake.

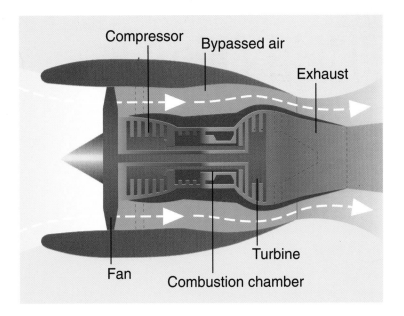

Compressor Bypassed air

Exhaust

Fan Combustion chamber Turbine

Before it escapes, the expanded air turns a bladed device called a turbine. This turns a large bladed compressor at the front of the engine, which helps keep the cycle of air going.

On engines called high-ratio bypass turbofans, a large fan is mounted at the front. More than 80 percent of the air sucked in at the front goes around, or bypasses, the central parts of the engine. The fan works almost like a propeller, as the bypass air delivers three-quarters of the thrust of the engine. The bypass air also wraps around the hot air coming from the exhaust. This acts as a silencer, making modern engines far quieter than older ones.

Modern turbofan engines are incredibly efficient and reliable, but they do not come cheap. Buying one for a jumbo jet costs around $6 million.

Diagram showing the parts of a high-ratio bypass turbofan engine.

An RAF Tornado takes off with its afterburners blazing against the dark rain clouds.

Afterburners

Fast military jets are equipped with afterburners. These inject fuel into the exhaust, producing flames, noise, and useful extra thrust. Afterburners eat up fuel at an alarming rate. Some jets can burn their entire fuel load in just ten minutes when their afterburners are used. Older military jets need afterburners for takeoff, but otherwise they are used only in combat where the extra power may make the difference between shooting down the enemy or being shot down themselves.

FLIGHT CONTROL

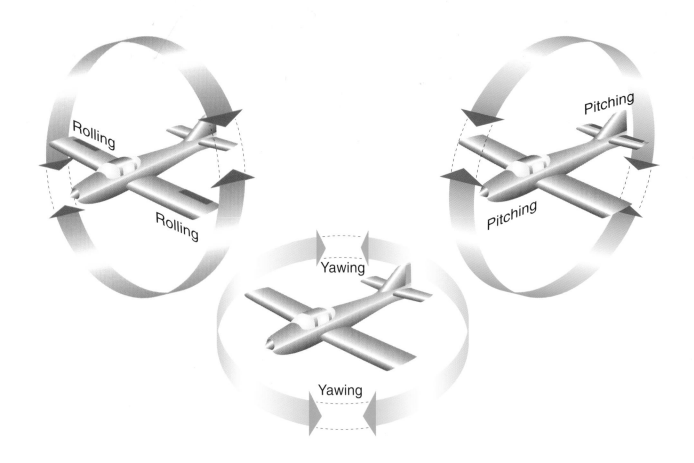

Rolling

Rolling

Pitching

Pitching

Yawing

Yawing

The main movements an aircraft can make are rolling, pitching, and yawing. The control surfaces used in each of these movements are highlighted.

All aircraft make three main movements: left and right, called yawing; up and down, called pitching; and rolling from side to side, called rolling (see diagram). These movements are controlled using movable parts, called control surfaces, on the wings and tail. The yaw is controlled by the rudder, the pitch by the elevators, and the roll by the ailerons.

Pilots move rudder pedals with their feet to control the rudder and the yaw. By moving the control column forward and backward, they control the elevator and the pitch of the aircraft. And by moving the control column sideways they control the ailerons, which make the aircraft roll. To make even a simple turn without losing altitude, all three movements have to be controlled at the same time.

The Wright heritage

Orville Wright

Wilbur Wright

The Wright brothers, Orville and Wilbur, designed the engine, propeller, and body, or airframe, for the world's first powered aircraft. Other aircraft inventors were close to flying their aircraft, but they did not fully understand the problems of controlling their machines had they become airborne.

The greatest achievement of the Wright brothers was their careful study of flight control. Through experiments with gliders, they realized that an aircraft has to be controlled around three axes, in pitch, yaw, and roll. The Wright brothers did not see the controls as something just to keep the aircraft balanced, but to be used to guide the aircraft through maneuvers. The Wright brothers established the basic principles of flight control for all aircraft.

Automatic pilot

In a modern airliner, takeoff and landing are usually under the control of the pilot, but for most of the rest of the flight, the automatic pilot does the work. The automatic pilot is a device that keeps the aircraft on a preset course. It does this far more accurately than any human could do and allows the pilot to spend his or her time checking the dials and switches in the cockpit. These instruments show how the aircraft's various systems are performing and warn of any failure or problems.

The large number of instruments may make it look as if monitoring is a difficult task but, in fact, this is done according to preset routines or procedures. On the left-hand side of the picture (right) are instruments giving basic but vital information on the aircraft's four engines. They are arranged in rows of four. As long as all four needles point in the same direction, the pilot can tell at a glance that all four engines are working well.

A pilot banks his jumbo jet as it climbs over Brisbane in Australia soon after takeoff. The jumbo jet is a highly complex piece of machinery, but it is being controlled according to the same basic principles as a small aircraft. The autopilot will fly the aircraft for most of the seven hours to Singapore.

GENERAL AVIATION

Around the world

In 1986, the ultimate do-it-yourself aircraft, *Voyager*, landed at Edwards Air Force Base in the Mojave Desert in California. It was the first and only aircraft to fly around the world nonstop without refueling. The flight lasted nine days and the two crew members, Dick Rutan and Jeana Yeager, showed the world what creative minds are capable of if they are allowed to experiment.

General aviation is the term used to describe all the various forms of small aircraft that are flown. Small aircraft can be put to many different uses, such as for enjoyment, as a sport, and for business.

Flying for fun

Flying is an enjoyable experience and many people fly just for the thrill they get out of it. The simplest aircraft are hang gliders and small hang glider-like powered aircraft called ultralights.

In Europe, the high cost of flying prevents most people from owning small aircraft. In some countries, such as the United States and Australia, flying is less expensive, so it is more common for people to own a small aircraft.

Some people build their own light aircraft from kits or plans. Some even design their own. Laws in the United States make it quite easy to fly your own experimental aircraft, so that is where many of the most interesting designs have been built.

John Stamper of Penrith in England built this light aircraft, called a Cozy, himself. The Cozy is a good example of an inventive home-built design. Home-builders like to get together at "fly-ins" to compare their aircraft and exchange ideas. At such fly-ins owners usually sleep under the wing of their aircraft in a small tent.

Air sports

Gliding is a comparatively cheap way of flying and popular with many people. Gliders used to be simple aircraft. Today, they are highly sophisticated machines.

Gliders do not have engines. They are pulled up into the air by a winch or by a powered aircraft. Once high enough, the towing rope is released and the challenge for the pilot is to stay airborne and fly as far as possible. If the pilot finds rising air currents called thermals, he or she can soar to great altitudes. One sporting event with gliders is to fly a certain route as fast as possible. To do so, glider pilots must fly from thermal to thermal on their way to the goal.

Aerobatics is perhaps the most challenging air sport of all. Pilots have to fly their powered light aircraft through all kinds of loops, rolls, and other spectacular maneuvers in order to win a competition. Landing and navigation competitions are also popular with owners of light aircraft.

Gliders are pulled up into the air by a winch or a powered aircraft.

The metal sheets making up the body of this Grumman Tiger light aircraft are glued instead of riveted together. This gives a smoother surface, lower fuel consumption, and greater speed.

HISTORIC AIRCRAFT

Historic aircraft are often flown by museums, clubs, or private owners at airshows or on the anniversary of an important event. They are also flown purely for the sheer excitement of flying something completely different.

One of the most popular types of veteran biplanes flying today is the de Havilland Tiger Moth. Here members of the Tiger Moth Diamond Nine Team are preparing for takeoff.

When sitting in the open cockpit of a Tiger Moth biplane during a 112-mph (180-kph) dive, you get much more sensation of speed than when flying in the quiet luxury of a 550-mph (900-kph) jet airliner. The noise from the propeller and the rush of the air in your face makes the Tiger Moth flight an experience not to miss.

The graceful Spitfire

Many people believe the Spitfire is the most beautiful aircraft ever built. Like other high-powered old fighters, the Spitfire is far more difficult to take off and land than modern aircraft. But once in the sky it is a sheer pleasure to fly.

Only 50 Spitfires are still flying—mostly in Great Britain and the United States. This one is flown by its owner, Carolyn Grace. During World War II, her Spitfire flew no less than 176 operations and was flown by French, Polish, Belgian, Norwegian, and New Zealand pilots. After the war it was converted to a two-seat trainer. Today, Carolyn flies it regularly at airshows. When it streaks past with a mighty roar from its Rolls-Royce engine, the crowd can appreciate the aircraft that played an important part in the history of the 20th century and marvel at the sight of its being put gracefully through its paces.

Warbirds

The term "warbirds" is used for historic military aircraft. Most warbirds are from World War II, but others are from the early years of the Cold War (see page 9). Fast, high-powered warbirds are very popular performers at airshows. They are also extremely expensive to fly—a Spitfire costs up to $6,400 per hour, for example. Most warbirds are kept flying by sponsorship and great voluntary efforts by people who enjoy working on these exciting old aircraft.

COMMERCIAL USES

Piper Saratogas used by a U.S. flying school.

Many pilots start their flying career in a small, single-engined, two-seater aircraft, such as the Cessna 150. The low cost of flying training in the United States and Australia makes it attractive to learn to fly there. Some of the biggest flying schools are found in these countries.

Flying small aircraft is often the first job professional pilots have. They may become flying instructors and train others to fly, or they may spend the summer taking vacationers on short pleasure flights.

Professional pilots might go on to fly twin-engined aircraft, known as "twins." Twins are used as "flying taxis" or by large companies for business trips.

Flying in the wilderness

In Australia, the Flying Doctor Service uses small aircraft to provide medical services for small towns in remote country areas. In places such as Alaska and Canada, there are such great distances to cover across the wilderness that often flying is the only realistic option.

A Grumman Widgeon flying boat in Central Alaska. These aircraft can land on and take off from lakes and rivers and are used to ferry passengers to remote places.

Private pilot's license — the first step

Camilla Christiansen is congratulated by her instructor after passing the test for her private pilot's license. This is a memorable occasion because she can now claim, "I'm a pilot." The license allows Camilla to fly single-engined aircraft for leisure. However, Camilla's ambitions go beyond this. After years of hard study and flight training, she hopes to become a professional pilot— then perhaps to fly small twins in different countries around the world. Later she may try to get a job with a large airline. For the moment, though, she believes it would be boring just to push buttons in the cockpit of a big jet. Perhaps the sky is the limit, but her license is Camilla's first major step.

Camilla learned to fly on a Cessna 150. Across the world, this aircraft is one of the most popular for flying training.

AIRCRAFT AND WILDLIFE

Some aircraft used for wildlife surveys are highly specialized, but for studies such as nest counting or surveying small lakes nothing beats an old Piper Cub. The observers have an excellent view from the cockpit and the aircraft's low speed helps, too.

Light, general-aviation aircraft are used to study wildlife. Counting birds at 100 mph (160 kph) has its limitations though, for it is almost impossible to spot small groups of rare birds. On the other hand, some bird-counting jobs can only be done from aircraft, for example, a huge flock of birds—perhaps extending for over 15 mi. (25 km) and numbering over 800,000 birds—flying over the sea.

Aircraft also provide a fast means of getting a more general view of large numbers of birds—often it is impossible to establish the exact number of birds, but the experienced observer will get a fairly good idea. From the observations, scientists can understand the movements of birds and how human activity, such as building bridges, affects them. In recent years, many bird sanctuaries have been established on the basis of surveys made from aircraft.

Whales and caribou

The U.S. Department of Fish and Game use light aircraft in their extensive research programs. Every year in June, thousands of white whales gather at Point Lay in northwest Alaska. The whales are photographed from the air, and later the pictures are analyzed to establish how the whale population is changing.

In the autumn, over 475,000 caribou (a type of reindeer) move south from their summer feeding grounds in the north of Alaska to escape the harsh winter. They move north again in the spring when warmer weather returns. Their migration route had been studied from the air and pilots were able to show the areas where the Trans-Alaskan oil pipeline had to be raised on pillars so that the caribou could pass underneath it on their journey.

Alaskan caribou make spectacular migrations, traveling up to 500 mi. (800 km) on their annual journeys. The only practical way of studying the route they take is from the air.

Pollution control

The North Sea alone is polluted by up to 300,000 tons of oil a year. Using very sensitive equipment, it is possible for aircraft to detect and measure the thickness and the extent of an oil slick. Between 1986 and 1996, aircraft from the German navy reported 1,642 cases of pollution. In 152 cases, they found the polluters, too. Military aircraft from many nations frequently train over the sea. They report any cases of pollution they have spotted.

The DC-3 is one of the most successful aircraft of all time—a total of 10,654 were built, the last one in 1947. This DC-3 is still in use and is fitted with a tail-mounted spraybar for breaking up oil slicks.

Air Atlantique at Coventry Airport in England operates seven DC-3s equipped to spray chemicals onto oil slicks that result from accidents, such as tankers running aground. Fortunately, such aircraft are rarely needed, but they are kept at constant readiness just in case.

AIRLINERS

A passenger on an international flight has her luggage checked by a customs officer before she is allowed into the country.

In 1958, for the first time more people crossed the Atlantic Ocean by air than by sea. Today, apart from ocean liners that carry tourists on cruises, not many people travel by ship over long distances—airliners are faster and much cheaper. The large airports, such as Kennedy Airport in New York and Great Britain's London Heathrow, are like crossroads, where people from many different continents meet.

Commuter aircraft

Commuter aircraft, or "commuters," are economical, small airliners that operate over short distances. The development of these aircraft has made it possible for the smaller airports to offer regular air services to customers. For example, in the United States, commuters are able to fly to and from a large number of small airports, such as Hibbing, MN; Mason City, IL; and Eau Claire, WI. These airports are so small that they will probably never receive longer domestic or intercontinental flights. But commuters make it possible for passengers from these places to get to big airports, such as Minneapolis-St.Paul, quickly.

The Jetstream is a highly successful commuter aircraft which is built in Scotland. Jetstreams serve the commuter lines from Minneapolis-St. Paul in the United States.

The United States is regarded as the birthplace of the commuter airliner, and it has a large number of companies in operation. But commuters are becoming increasingly important in Europe, Australia, and the Far East, too.

Helicopters are a comfortable and efficient way of transporting workers to oil rigs in the often stormy and hostile North Sea.

Helicopters

Helicopters are noisier, slower, and far more expensive to operate than fixed-wing aircraft. But they do have the unique ability to hover and land on the same spot. They often have special uses, such as ferrying workers to oil platforms at sea, rescuing climbers trapped in the mountains, and carrying TV cameras during the coverage of sports events. Helicopters are also used as ambulances to carry critically ill people to the hospital and to land VIPs in the center of cities.

SAINT MARY'S SCHOOL
309 E. Chestnut Street
Lancaster, Ohio 43130

MEDIUM-RANGE AIRLINERS

A passenger has her ticket checked before boarding the aircraft. Airline check-in staff register all passengers before a flight.

Medium-range aircraft carry between 100 and 200 passengers and make up more than two-thirds of the total number of jet airliners ever produced (approximately 15,000). Each of the large U.S. airlines, such as United Airlines, Northwest Airlines, Delta Air Lines, American Airlines, and Continental Airlines, operates more than 300 medium-range jets, which is more than twice as many as any European airline. They fly a complicated network of routes all over the United States.

In Europe, medium-range jets fly millions of vacationers to Mediterranean resorts. They also connect major political, financial, and cultural centers, such as London, Amsterdam, Frankfurt, and Paris. These cities are all less than 90 minutes apart by air. Modern jets make it possible to have breakfast at home, a couple of meetings in a foreign city, and be back in time for supper.

Best-sellers

The Boeing 737 first flew in 1967 and is the best-selling airliner ever. In 1997, the delivery of number 3,000 by the jetliner manufacturer, Boeing, will almost coincide with the airliner's 30th anniversary. New models of the 737 will be flying well into the 21st century with improved engines, wings, and cockpit layouts. Other successful medium-range aircraft from Boeing are the 727 and 757.

McDonnell Douglas is another manufacturer of civil jetliners. This U.S. company has produced more than 2,000 DC-9s and MD-80s, and has plans to develop and improve these aircraft in the future.

Since the late 1970s, the joint European company, Airbus, has been in fierce competition with Boeing and McDonnell Douglas, producing such jetliners as the medium-range A-320.

An Airbus A-320 of Vietnam Airlines at Saigon Than Son Nhut Airport in front of shelters once used by U.S. warplanes. The fast growth of air traffic in Asia makes it likely that a medium-range airliner may be built in the Far East in the future.

A black box is checked before it is installed in an airliner.

The black box

Modern air travel is considerably safer than going for a drive in the family car. Nonetheless, all airliners are equipped with the so-called black box, which monitors all communications in the cockpit and every movement of the aircraft. In the unlikely case of an accident, the information the black box records helps the crash investigators in their efforts to discover the cause of the disaster. Once the reason is found, airlines all over the world may have to make modifications to their aircraft to prevent the same accident from happening again. In this way, the black box is an important piece of equipment in the improvement of safety. To make it easy to find on a crash site it is, in fact, orange not black.

LONG HAUL

During the 50 years leading to World War I, no less than 34 million Europeans emigrated to the United States. For many, the cost of the ticket on the steamship left them penniless, and most migrants were never able to return to the "old country."

The introduction of large, wide-bodied jet airliners in the 1970s started another travel revolution. Only this time fares dropped so low that it became a realistic option for many to travel between continents for their vacations. The big jets made possible what the migrants a century before had not even dared to dream of.

Jumbo jets

On its maiden flight in 1969, the Boeing 747 became the world's first big jet airliner—it could fly up to 4,100 mi. (6,700 km) with 374 passengers on board. Since then, the jumbo jet has been steadily improved and now flies almost twice as far and with up to 20 percent more passengers—in one seating arrangement, 660 passengers can be packed in like sardines. It is still the world's largest jet airliner. Jumbo jets perform more than 1,000 flights across the Pacific Ocean each week, which is more than 75 percent of all Pacific air traffic.

With 34 in service, Singapore Airlines is the world's leading operator of the Boeing 747-400— the latest high-tech version of the jumbo jet.

A Delta Airlines Boeing 767 arrives at Oslo in Norway after a transatlantic flight.

The Lockheed Tristar and the McDonnell Douglas DC-10 and MD11 are other important big jet airliners. Airbus has recently challenged the U.S. manufacturers with the latest Airbus A-330 and A-340 jet airliners.

On two engines across the Atlantic

When the 210-seat Boeing 767 airliner was introduced in 1982, it represented a breakthrough in aircraft technology. Jet engines had now become so reliable that it was considered safe to carry passengers across the Atlantic Ocean on just two engines—in the past, in case of engine failure, only three- or four-jet engine airliners were considered safe for the long-haul flight from the United States to Europe.

The 767 is now by far the most used aircraft on the important North Atlantic Ocean route. It has made it possible to offer nonstop flights between cities that do not carry enough air traffic to justify the larger jumbo jet.

Taking a break

Members of the cabin crew prepare to relax for a few hours in the rest area above the passenger cabin in the tail of a 747-400 jumbo jet. The nonstop flight between Singapore and London takes 14 hours, and the crew must rest in order to be alert to the needs of the passengers and to assist them should an emergency occur.

CARGO

Containers being loaded into the forward cargo compartment under the passenger cabin on a jumbo jet at Singapore's Changi Airport.

Airmail rather than passengers helped the early airlines to establish themselves. Cargo is still an important source of money for all the world's airlines—between them they carry more than 25,000 tons of cargo every day. Some cargo is flown in aircraft specially built for the job. However, the cargo compartments on the big passenger jets are huge, and can hold much more than just luggage. The extra cargo they carry helps make flights economical.

Flying cargo is certainly more expensive than transporting it on ships or railroads. Air cargo, therefore, tends to be of high value. Cargo can be gold, programs for computers, or essential spare parts needed for important machinery. Some fruits and other goods that are delicate or become stale or rot quickly have to reach their destination quickly, and aircraft are the only practical way of transporting them. Racehorses and rare zoo animals are also sent by air over long distances.

The Boeing 747-400F is a pure freighter version of the jumbo jet and so has no need for windows. This one, about to take off at Melbourne Airport in Australia, is operated by Hong Kong-based Cathay Pacific Airways.

Old or new?

Instead of being scrapped, some older passenger aircraft are used to fly cargo. For example, old turboprop aircraft are kept busy flying flowers and vegetables from the Channel Islands to the British mainland. The aircraft are well maintained, and one has logged more than 38,000 hours in the air.

Older types of jet aircraft are being converted to cargo planes, too. It is much cheaper to buy and convert an old jumbo jet than to buy a freighter straight from the factory. But a new aircraft might burn 15 percent less fuel, which could be a saving of more than 3,300 lbs (1,500 kg) of fuel per hour. It will also have a better range and lower maintenance costs. For these reasons, some airliners invest in the latest cargo aircraft.

An old Handley Page Herald of Channel Express at Guernsey Airport. It is used to transport flowers and vegetables to Great Britain.

MILITARY AIRCRAFT

The Sea Harrier is the naval version of the Harrier—a modern fighter that can take off and land vertically. In the United States, the Harrier has seen service with the marines.

"If you want peace, prepare for war." This saying from Roman times sums up the logic behind the arms race during the Cold War—potential enemies should be frightened off from even considering an attack (see page 9). With much improved East–West relations in recent years, many countries have cut their defense spending and withdrawn older military aircraft from service.

Most leaders consider war to be an unacceptable way of solving problems between nations. However, some are willing to take up arms to get what they want—be it revenge, oil, wealth, or land. As a result, most nations have military forces, which they will use to defend themselves against attack from an unfriendly country.

Aircraft roles

Today's military aircraft carry out the same basic roles established during World War I, that is, gathering information about the enemy; bombing communications systems, weapons, and soldiers; and shooting down enemy aircraft. Some modern aircraft, such as the F-16, are able to perform all three roles.

Many more types of missions are flown by today's military aircraft. Transports fly supplies or drop soldiers by parachute. Helicopters may evacuate the wounded or be equipped to destroy tanks or submarines. So-called Wild Weasel fighters locate and destroy enemy radar sites.

The limitations of air power

The war in Vietnam (1964–1975) between South Vietnam (supported by the United States) and the communist Vietcong (supported by North Vietnam) became a tragic demonstration of the limitations of air power. During the war, U.S. aircraft dropped more bombs on an area the size of Italy than had been used in Europe during the whole of World War II. The bombs caused much destruction but, in this confused war, it was very difficult to tell friend from foe, and many civilians were killed. The air war helped to turn world opinion against U.S. involvement in the Vietnam War, and most U.S. forces were withdrawn by 1973.

One of the world's most capable air-to-air fighters is the McDonnell Douglas F-15 Eagle. F-15s have taken part in both the Gulf War and air operations over Bosnia. These U.S. Air Force F-15s are part of the air defense of Alaska.

Keeping the peace?

However, other modern conflicts have proved that air power can be decisive if the reason for military action is clear and the military targets are well defined. Since 1990, the air forces of the United States, Great Britain, and a number of other nations have been actively engaged in war operations on behalf of the United Nations (UN).

For example, the Gulf War (1990–1991) was fought to force the occupying Iraqi force out of Kuwait. A massive air campaign under U.S. command practically won the war single-handedly. Since then the British Royal Air Force (RAF) has been busy protecting the Kurds in northern Iraq.

More recently, in the tragic war in Bosnia, air operations have been an important factor in protecting civilians. In the end, a bombing campaign on behalf of the UN forced the sides to negotiate peace.

REACHING THE TARGET

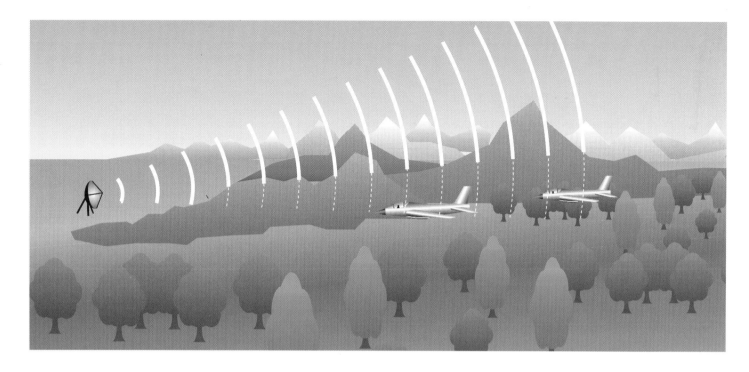

Radar beams travel in straight lines. Staying low helps aircraft hide from enemy radar.

Modern military aircraft are among the most sophisticated weapons ever invented. But the defenses they are up against are highly complex, too. For example, a pilot is given the task of photographing some enemy installations. He will not attack the installations, but the flight is by no means peaceful. If the photographs reveal an important military target, bombers will soon follow. So the pilot must expect to be shot at just as if he were flying a bomber.

Tanker aircraft

Air-to-air refueling has become an essential part of modern air operations. Attacking aircraft can take off with their heavy load of extra bombs only if they are not fully fueled. Often this means that they must refuel in the air before flying on to their target. Over enemy territory they might have to engage in air combat and use their afterburners to get out of trouble. This could well mean that they would not have enough fuel to reach their home base. So a visit to a tanker aircraft on the way home will be necessary, too. Tanker aircraft were vital for the air operations in both the Vietnam War and the Gulf War.

An F-16 receives fuel from a KC-130 tanker during a military exercise.

Flying low at high speed demands the highest concentration from the pilot.

Usually a pilot will fly close to the ground in order to avoid being detected by radar. Should enemy radar detect him, equipment in the cockpit will warn him that this has happened. If the enemy fires radar-controlled missiles at him, the pilot has two means of self-defense, called chaff and the jammer. Chaff are tiny strips of tinfoil that confuse the enemy's radar picture, while the jammer emits signals that prevent the clear reception of the radar signals.

These defenses are useless against infrared missiles. If one of these is fired, it will home in on the fighter by locking onto its hot exhaust. To prevent being shot down, the pilot may fire flares for the missile to follow instead.

If all else fails, the pilot will try to out-turn the missile. If he turns hard at the right moment, the missile will streak past the aircraft and run out of fuel.

Other hazards are machine-gun fire from the ground or attack by enemy fighters. Good training and the best equipment will help the pilot reach his target and get the photographs. But as always in war, luck plays an important part in staying alive.

RADAR

The AWACS' radar can detect flying aircraft in any direction up to 310 mi. (500 km) away.

The first time radar played a decisive role in air warfare was during the Battle of Britain in 1940. The British fighters were greatly outnumbered by German aircraft, but radar helped the British fighters be in the right place in the sky at the right time.

During the later part of World War II, airborne radar helped British and U.S. bombers to find their way in the night skies over Germany. But the Germans used the radar beams to pinpoint the position of the bombers and attack them. Meanwhile, jammers were used by the British and U.S. forces to interfere with the pictures on the German radar.

Air battles had become an electronic game of hide-and-seek in which survival depended as much on electronics as on raw courage. Since the development of radar, the use of electronic equipment has become a vital part of modern warfare.

AWACS

The Boeing E3 Sentry is often simply called AWACS (Airborne Warning and Control System). An AWACS is basically a Boeing 707 with a 30-ft. (9-m) diameter radar mounted on the top. A specialist team working in the windowless body of the aircraft, or fuselage, uses the radar to spot enemy aircraft and guide friendly aircraft toward them. The AWACS is unarmed, but its ability to control an air battle makes it the most important plane in the sky—or the most dangerous if you happen to be the enemy.

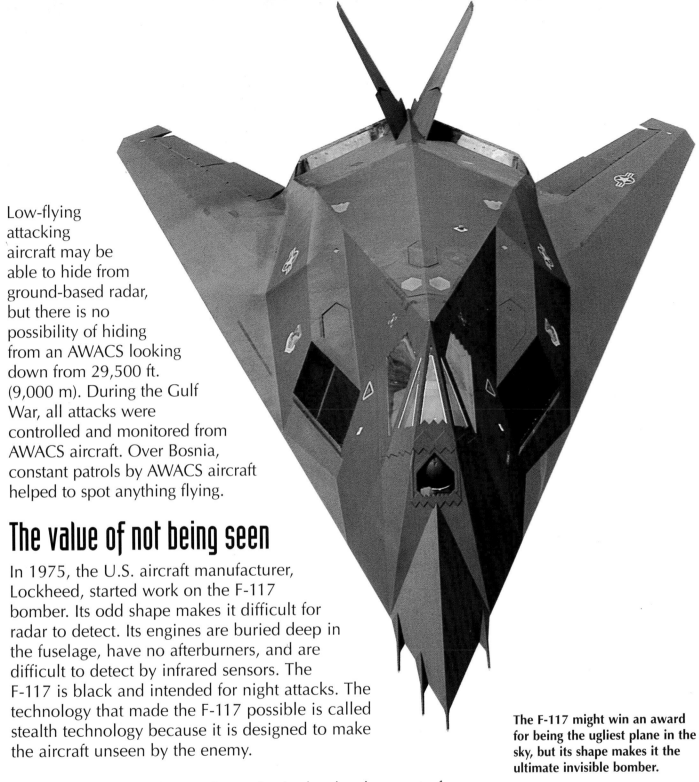

Low-flying attacking aircraft may be able to hide from ground-based radar, but there is no possibility of hiding from an AWACS looking down from 29,500 ft. (9,000 m). During the Gulf War, all attacks were controlled and monitored from AWACS aircraft. Over Bosnia, constant patrols by AWACS aircraft helped to spot anything flying.

The value of not being seen

In 1975, the U.S. aircraft manufacturer, Lockheed, started work on the F-117 bomber. Its odd shape makes it difficult for radar to detect. Its engines are buried deep in the fuselage, have no afterburners, and are difficult to detect by infrared sensors. The F-117 is black and intended for night attacks. The technology that made the F-117 possible is called stealth technology because it is designed to make the aircraft unseen by the enemy.

The F-117 might win an award for being the ugliest plane in the sky, but its shape makes it the ultimate invisible bomber.

The F-117 was a major turning point in the development of military aircraft because it made air defense radar useless. In the Gulf War, F-117s penetrated strong Iraqi defenses, hitting key targets with astounding precision. In 1,271 missions not a single F-117 was lost. It is difficult to shoot down an aircraft you do not know is there.

MILITARY TRANSPORTS

In June 1948, the Soviet Union cut off road, railroad, and canal links between the western sector of the city of Berlin and West Germany to try and force it to give up its independent status. In more than 200,000 flights, U.S. and British transport aircraft supplied the city with food and fuel. More than half the weight of the supplies flown in was coal to heat the houses during the winter. These flights became known as the Berlin Airlift, and they were so successful that, by May 1949, the Soviet authorities were forced to give up their blockade.

A Hercules performs a low-level drop of supplies. This aircraft is one of the most successful ever built. The first was flown in 1954, and new ones are still coming off the production line. The Hercules can carry a heavy load and still land on a small, dirt airstrip. Should the airstrip be in a combat zone, the aircraft will take a lot of damage and still get out again.

Humanitarian flights

Military transport aircraft are still being used today. Some are flying aid in emergency situations on behalf of the UN. During the war in Bosnia, cargo aircraft flew supplies to Saravejo and other towns and cities under siege to lessen the suffering of the civilian population. Flights were often risky, and the crew usually flew dressed in bulletproof vests.

"A Sarajevo landing" has become a standard term in the language of military pilots. This is a landing with a very steep approach to lessen the risk of being hit by gunfire from the ground.

In Ethiopia, military transports saved thousands of lives during the famine of 1984–1985. The Soviet Union, Germany, France, Italy, Libya, Poland, and Great Britain flew large numbers of supplies to starving communities around the country. Flying was often the only way to get the food where it was needed. The RAF used the Hercules aircraft for a grand total of 2,152 famine-relief flights. Almost half the food was dropped from the air because the aircraft could not always find a place to land.

The growing number of peacekeeping operations around the world makes the ability to transport soldiers and equipment rapidly by aircraft ever more important.

Search and rescue

Search and Rescue (SAR) flights are performed by helicopters from many countries. In Great Britain, military helicopters rescued more than 1,300 people during 1995. The job of rescuing people at sea can be quite hazardous. One crew-member, the winchman, is usually lowered to help lift a person from a stricken ship or a drifting liferaft. In calm weather, this presents few problems. But the winchman may have to do it at night in a howling gale over mountainous waves.

THE FUTURE

Eurofighter is a joint British, German, Italian, and Spanish project.

During World War I, aircraft were designed, tested, and proven in combat within weeks. Today, this process usually takes more than ten years. For example, early experiments on the Eurofighter began in 1982, and it may go into service in the year 2000.

Affordability

The RAF originally planned to buy 250 Eurofighters, but now it has settled for around 230. "Affordability" has become an important word when deciding what modern military aircraft to buy—there is no point in ordering superfighters if you cannot afford to pay for them.

The design of the F-22 has benefited from Lockheed´s experience with stealth technology.

Lockheed—the company that developed the revolutionary F-117—has applied its stealth technology to the extremely capable F-22 fighter. When approaching an enemy aircraft, the F-22 is a hundred times more difficult to detect on radar than the F-15 that it is going to replace. But good as it is, the F-22 is also extremely expensive. The U.S. Air Force originally wanted 750, with the first aircraft going into service in 1994. Now 400 F-22s, with a delivery date of 2003, seems more realistic.

Future stealth

The Eurofighter will not be very stealthy, because its basic design dates back to before the time when technology made stealth possible. Since then, the success of the F-117 has clearly demonstrated the value of stealth. So research has already begun to design a new generation of military combat aircraft.

Early models for testing show radical new shapes and control systems to make them invisible to radar. These aircraft may go into service after 2010—if nations need and can afford to buy and fly such aircraft.

An artist's impression of a future combat aircraft under development by a U.S.–British team. The aircraft will be able to land and take off vertically like the Harrier and have a stealth design, which will make it invisible to radar.

Future airliners

The 20th century has seen a steady growth in civil air traffic, and it is most likely this will continue. Boeing estimates a worldwide need for more than 3,000 new medium-range airliners by the turn of the century.

The fastest growth will probably be in the Far East. The economies there are growing faster than anywhere else. By the year 2010, the Asia–Pacific region may account for more than half the world's air traffic. Some countries in Asia now want to start producing a medium-range airliner. In the future, one may team up with an established company to produce the first joint U.S.–Asian or Euro–Asian airliner.

LARGER AIRCRAFT?

A3XX is the Airbus proposal for an airliner that will carry more than 550 passengers. Being just a little larger than a jumbo jet, it could use existing terminals at airports. The A3XX would be a genuine double-decker, as this picture shows.

Major airports are limited by the number of aircraft they can handle—at peak times they are stretched to the limit of their capacity. One way to cater to more passengers is to build even larger aircraft.

Plans exist to build airliners that will seat 800 to 1,000 passengers. Boeing and Airbus have considered producing one together in order to share the huge development costs. But it seems more likely that Boeing will develop the jumbo jet into even bigger and more advanced versions, while Airbus will go ahead with its A3XX, which could then be the world's largest passenger aircraft. Another solution is to build new runways and points of access for passengers and cargo. For example, at London Heathrow, Terminal 5 is being planned to take its first passengers in 2002. It will be designed to cope with the flow of more than 800 passengers traveling on tomorrow's aircraft.

Faster aircraft?

Concorde is still the world's only supersonic passenger aircraft, but although beautiful, exciting, and a technical masterpiece, Concorde was also a financial disaster. There is no doubt that passengers like to get to their destinations fast, but not necessarily at the sky-high prices demanded for flights on Concorde.

Despite this, large aircraft manufacturers are carrying out studies into tomorrow's supersonic transports. The aircraft will have to be bigger than Concorde, fly farther, and be more friendly to the environment—not least in terms of noise pollution. Also the cost of flying should be about the same as flying on other types of aircraft. These requirements make it unlikely that a successor to Concorde will appear in the near future.

A Boeing design for a successor to Concorde. However, it is likely that larger rather than faster aircraft will be built in the near future.

Toward the 21st century

Never in history have so many people traveled so far, so fast, and at such low prices. The development of aircraft has been one of the great success stories of the 20th century. And all indications are that flying will become an even more widespread means of transportation in the 21st century.

Other recent inventions, such as telecommunications and computers, have made the world seem a smaller place, too. Using virtual reality, you can travel to different parts of the world in your own living room. But why settle for second best? Aircraft offer the chance to travel to fascinating parts of the world and to actually see, smell, hear, and feel the real world in person.

DATE CHART

1903 The Wright brothers fly the world's first, powered, heavier-than-air aircraft at Kill Devil Hills, south of Kitty Hawk in North Carolina.

1909 French pilot Louis Bleriot makes the first crossing of the English Channel in an aircraft.

1919 The Vickers Vimy is involved in several record-breaking flights: the first nonstop flight across the Atlantic Ocean; the first England–Australia flight; and the first England–Cape Town flight (using two Vimys that crashed on the way).

1925 The first flight of the de Havilland Moth. The simplicity and reliability of this aircraft makes it one of the most popular private aircraft. Various types of Moths—Gipsy Moth, Hornet Moth, Leopard Moth, and Tiger Moth—are used for many record-breaking flights.

1927 Charles Lindbergh makes the first solo flight between New York and Paris—an event that captures the imagination of the world. His plane, "The Spirit of St. Louis,"

can be seen at the National Air and Space Museum in Washington, D.C.

1928 Charles Kingsford Smith and his crew make the first flight across of the Pacific Ocean in his aircraft, a Fokker F.VII-3m named *Southern Cross*.

1935 First flight by the Douglas DC-3—the "Jumbo" of its day. The DC-3 immediately establishes itself as a world leader in commercial aviation. During World War II, it becomes the most important cargo plane and troop carrier for the Allies.

1939 The world's first jet aircraft, the Heinkel He 178, is flown in Germany.

1945 Two nuclear bombs are dropped on Hiroshima and Nagasaki in Japan by B-29 bomber aircraft.

1947 U.S. test pilot Chuck Yeager breaks the sound barrier in the rocket-powered experimental X-1.

1949 The de Havilland Comet becomes the world's first jet-powered airliner.

1954 The first flight of the Lockheed F-104 Starfighter—the first combat aircraft capable of flying at twice the speed of sound.

1966 The Harrier becomes the world's first combat aircraft capable of vertical takeoff and landing—a milestone in the development of military aircraft.

1969 Concorde flies for the first time. A Boeing 747 jumbo jet is flown for the first time, heralding a new era of mass travel.

1977 The first flight of the "Have Blue"—a research aircraft that will lead to the Lockheed F-117 stealth bomber—the first military aircraft that cannot be seen on radar.

1982 The Boeing 767 is introduced. Although flown all over the world, the twin-engined airliner is today the most important aircraft on the route over the North Atlantic.

1986 Jeana Yeager and Dick Rutan become the first and so far the only people to fly nonstop around the world without refueling. The flight lasts nine days. Their aircraft, *Voyager,* which they helped to build, can be seen today in the National Air and Space Museum in Washington, D.C.

1991 First flight of the Airbus 340—the largest aircraft built in Europe and the first European aircraft to challenge the U.S. dominance in the big jet long-haul market.

GLOSSARY

aloft In the air.

altitude The height of an aircraft above the ground or above sea level.

aviators People involved in the flying of an aircraft, for example, pilots, navigators, and flight engineers.

banks To "lean" an aircraft to one side as it goes into a turn.

Battle of Britain An aerial battle fought in the skies over Great Britain during the summer and autumn of 1940. The German attackers tried to destroy the RAF and clear the way for an invasion of England but failed.

biplane An aircraft with two sets of wings, one above the other, for example, a Tiger Moth or a Vickers Vimy.

blockade To surround a city or a country so that food, fuel, and other supplies cannot reach it.

cabin crew The stewardesses and stewards working in the cabin of a passenger aircraft. The most important function of the cabin crew is to be ready to help the passengers in emergency situations. However, they spend most of their time serving drinks and food and attending to the passengers' other needs.

civilian Nonmilitary.

cockpit The small compartment in an aircraft from which the pilot controls the flight. In large aircraft, the cockpit is sometimes known as the "flight deck."

cruising Flying from one point to another, usually at a constant speed and altitude.

domestic Of one's own country; not foreign.

exhaust The parts of an engine through which waste gases escape; also the gases themselves.

formation A group of aircraft flying together.

intercontinental Able to travel, or fly, between two continents.

maiden flight The first flight of an aircraft.

maneuvers The planned movements of an aircraft in flight. At airshows, aircraft often perform loops and rolls for the crowd.

military Relating to a country's armed forces.

navigation The art of finding one's way from one point to another. Early aviators often navigated by following railroad lines. Modern navigation uses computers and satellites to pinpoint an aircraft's position, heading, and time to destination.

piston engines Engines that have parts that slide back and forth inside a hollow cylinder.

radar (RAdio Detecting And Ranging) A method of detecting aircraft, using radio waves, which bounce back off the aircraft and form a picture of it on a screen.

replica An almost exact copy of an old aircraft. Modern engines and other important parts make replicas safer to fly than the original old aircraft.

RAF Royal Air Force (the air forces of the British Commonwealth).

supersonic Able to fly faster than the speed of sound. Apart from Concorde, only military jets are designed to fly this fast.

tailwind A wind blowing in the same direction as the course of an aircraft.

trenches Long ditches dug for protection in wartime and sometimes fortified with sandbags. World War I was largely fought from trenches.

United Nations (UN) An organization of independent countries that promotes peace and international cooperation. It was formed in 1945.

virtual reality A world, created by computer, that has the appearance and effect of being real but, in fact, is not. Virtual reality games are now popular.

FIND OUT MORE

Books to read

Baines, Francesca. *Planes*. Wordwise. Danbury, CT: Franklin Watts, 1994.

Carter, Sharon. *Careers in Aviation*. Careers in Depth. New York: Rosen Group, 1989.

Dale, Henry. *Early Flying Machines*. Discoveries and Inventions. New York: Oxford University Press, 1993.

Gunning, Thomas G. *Dream Planes*. Parsippany, NJ: Silver Burdett Press, 1992.

Holland, Gini. *Airplanes*. Inventors and Inventions. Tarrytown, NY: Marshall Cavendish, 1995.

Jennings, Terry. *Planes, Gliders, Helicopters, and Other Flying Machines*. How Things Work. New York: Kingfisher Books, 1993.

Nahum, Andrew. *Flying Machines*. Eyewitness. New York: Knopf Books for Young Readers, 1990.

Sullivan, George. *How an Airport Really Works*. New York: Dutton Children's Books, 1993.

Places to visit

Many larger airports have spectators' platforms from where it is possible to get excellent views of aircraft landing and taking off.

National Air and Space Museum, Smithsonian Institution,
Sixth Street and Independence Avenue, Washington D.C., 20560
203-357-2700
Many exhibits about aircraft.

United States Air Force Museum,
Wright Patterson Air Force Base, Ohio
Many exhibits about military aircraft.

47

INDEX

© Copyright 1997 Wayland (Publishers) Ltd.